POP CULTURE BIOS

EMMA

STONE

STAR OF THE STAGE, TV, AND FILM

HEATHER E. SCHWARTZ

Lerner Publications Company

MINNEAPOLIS

To my glam grandma,
Grace Kanner

Lerner Publications Company
A division of Lerner Publishing Group, Inc.
241 First Avenue North
Minneapolis, MN 55401 U.S.A.

For reading levels and more information, look up this title at www.lernerbooks.com.

Library of Congress Cataloging-in-Publication Data

Schwartz, Heather E.
    Emma Stone : star of the stage, tv, and film / by Heather E. Schwartz.
        p.   cm. — (Pop culture bios)
    Includes index.
    ISBN 978-1-4677-1440-2 (lib. bdg. : alk. paper)
    ISBN 978-1-4677-2498-2 (eBook)
    1. Stone, Emma, 1988– Juvenile literature. 2. Actors—United States—Biography—Juvenile literature. 3. Singers—United States—Biography—Juvenile literature. I. Title.
PN2287.S73S385   2014
791.4302'8092—dc23
[B]   2013013633

Manufactured in the United States of America
1 – PC – 12/31/13

INTRODUCTION

PAGE 4

CHAPTER ONE
GIRL WITH A GOAL

PAGE 8

CHAPTER TWO
BREAKING IN

PAGE 14

CHAPTER THREE
LEADING LADY

PAGE 20

EMMA PICS!	28
SOURCE NOTE	30
MORE EMMA INFO	30
INDEX	31

INTRODUCTION

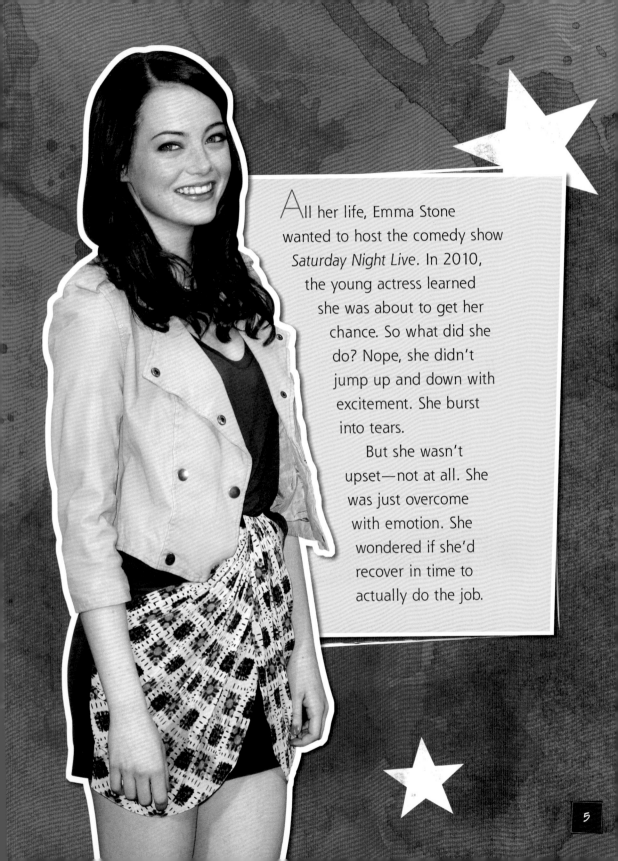

All her life, Emma Stone wanted to host the comedy show *Saturday Night Live*. In 2010, the young actress learned she was about to get her chance. So what did she do? Nope, she didn't jump up and down with excitement. She burst into tears.

But she wasn't upset—not at all. She was just overcome with emotion. She wondered if she'd recover in time to actually do the job.

She dialed up her friend Justin Timberlake (yes, *that* Justin Timberlake!), who'd hosted before. His advice: if she was going to cry on the show, fine—as long as she made it funny.

As it turned out, Emma didn't cry. She cracked up the audience, using stories from her own life to kick off the jokes.

Emma takes to the stage on Saturday Night Live.

"I've wanted to be on this stage since I was a little girl. That's why when I was 14, I convinced my parents to let me move to L.A. to pursue acting," she said during her opening monologue. "A few years later I was doing movies and a few years after that I'm here hosting *Saturday Night Live*. And it is truly a dream come true."

MONOLOGUE =
a solo speaking performance

Emma loved doing the skits for *Saturday Night Live*.

CHAPTER ONE

GIRL WITH A GOAL

Emma's hometown of Scottsdale, Arizona (ABOVE), is next to Arizona's capital, Phoenix.

Emma is one girl who knows how to get what she wants. It all started when she was growing up in Scottsdale, Arizona. Emily Jean (that's her real name!) was born on November 6, 1988. As a kid, she was noisy and bossy. Her role models? Loud, funny, famous guys, like Steve Martin and John Candy. She loved their movies and wanted to be just like them.

There was one hitch, though. When Emma was eight, she started having panic attacks. Out of nowhere, she'd suddenly be slammed with feelings of fear.

FAMILY MATTERS

Emma has one younger brother, Spencer (LEFT). She once took him as her date to an award ceremony. He made her promise to talk about him in her acceptance speech. She got lots of laughs when she did.

DREAM JOBS

As a kid, Emma loved computers. She even designed her own websites! She also loved writing. So she started an online magazine for girls. If she hadn't become an actor, she would've wanted to be a web designer or a journalist.

During the school day, she just wanted to go home. After school, she was scared to go to friends' houses to play. She didn't feel strong or confident. She felt sick. How was she supposed to become a famous funny girl?

Therapy helped, and so did acting. Emma liked getting onstage and making people laugh. It made her feel good. Soon Emma started believing in herself again. She was back to dreaming big. Sure, at first glance, she might not *look* like star material.

FUNNY GIRL

The first movie Emma remembers watching is *The Jerk*, starring Steve Martin (LEFT). It made her want to do comedy.

Emma wore braces
in sixth grade.

She wore glasses
and braces. She still
sucked her thumb. But
so what? She wasn't
about to let anything
get in her way.

The Acting Bug

Emma acted at a local youth theater. She also performed
in their comedy improv group. By the time she was twelve,
she was serious about acting. In fact, she wanted to leave
school to make more time for auditions. Most parents
probably wouldn't go for
that plan. And most kids
wouldn't have the guts to
ask. But Emma made sure
her mom and dad heard
her out.

She made a presentation on foam boards and convinced her parents to homeschool her.

The same year, Emma flew to Hollywood, in Los Angeles, to audition for a role on a Nickelodeon show. She didn't get the part. But she did learn one important lesson: This crazy city wasn't for her. She did *not* want to live in L.A.

"Project Hollywood" As a high school freshman, though, Emma changed her mind about Hollywood. It suddenly hit her: she couldn't spend the rest of her life in Scottsdale.

MAKING STUFF UP

Emma loved working on *The House Bunny* and *Superbad*—two films she later acted in—because she got to do improv in many of her scenes.

Emma decided in high school that she wanted to move out of her hometown.

Sure, she'd been in tons of local theater productions. But now she was ready to aim for the silver screen. And her hometown wasn't exactly Moviemaking Central. If she wanted a shot at a film career, she would *have* to move to L.A. And she would have to convince her parents it was the right thing to do.

So she created another presentation. After all, it had worked before! This time, she went high-tech. She used PowerPoint and added music—Madonna's song "Hollywood," of course! The finished product was called "Project Hollywood." She showed it to her parents and served them popcorn while they watched. The result: at the age of fifteen, Emma left home for Los Angeles.

Emma's mom (LEFT) headed to L.A. with the young actress to help Emma follow her dreams.

CHAPTER TWO

BREAKING IN

Emma has been both blonde (LEFT) and brunette (RIGHT).

Before she made it as a movie star, Emma worked part-time baking treats for dogs. She says she wasn't very good at it, though!

In 2004, Emma and her mom, Krista, moved into an apartment in L.A. For eight months, Emma tried out for roles. For eight months, she got rejected.

It was enough to make any girl feel as though she had a great big *L* stuck to her forehead. But when Emma couldn't take it anymore, she didn't quit. Instead, she made a bold change. The problem had nothing to do with her talents, she decided. The problem was her hair.

Dyeing for a Break

As a natural blonde, Emma often ended up auditioning for cheerleader roles. But she wasn't getting those parts. So she decided to try something new. She dyed her long locks dark brown. Maybe *that* would help.

Emma's husky voice sets her apart from other actresses. But do you know how she got it? As a baby, she cried a *lot*. She screamed so much that she damaged her vocal cords!

Soon after, Emma's mom found out about a VH1 reality show. It was actually a talent competition. Actors and actresses would compete for roles on a planned sitcom called *The New Partridge Family*—a reboot of a popular 1970s show. In the original show, the teenage character Laurie Partridge had brown hair. With her brand-new dye job, Emma had just the right look for that role.

Of course, looks aren't everything, even in Hollywood. The contestants were judged as actors and singers too. That's where Emma showed her true talents. She nailed her cover of Pat Benatar's "We Belong"—and won the competition!

COVER =
a performance of a song originally written and sung by someone else

Super Score

The New Partridge Family wasn't a hit. In fact, the show was canceled before it even aired. Emma must've been bummed. Or was she? By then, she was tight with the show's music producer. Through him, she met her lawyer. And through her lawyer, she met her manager, Doug Wald. Now she had a pro on her side. Doug could help her build a solid acting career.

> MANAGER =
> a person who helps guide an actor's career

First, she started getting roles on TV. She appeared on *Malcolm in the Middle* and the FOX show *Drive*.

Emma played a young driver in cross-country road races on the FOX show *Drive*.

Emma, shown here on set with Jonah Hill (LEFT), got a lot of laughs in her first movie, *Superbad*.

But it wasn't all easy breezy from then on. When Emma went for a major role on the NBC show *Heroes*, actress Hayden Panettiere beat her out.

That was a low point for Emma. But soon, she scored an even better part: the role of Jules in the movie *Superbad*.

NAME GAME

Emma started her acting career as Emily Stone. She switched to Riley Stone for a while. Finally, she decided to go with Emma, her mother's nickname for her.

Superbad was a huge hit. And Emma's comedic timing and natural beauty got a lot of attention.

But that was just the beginning. Between 2008 and 2009, she was in five more movies: *The Rocker*, *The House Bunny*, *Ghosts of Girlfriends Past*, *Zombieland*, and *Paper Man*. In 2010, she landed her first lead role, in the movie *Easy A*.

In *Easy A*, Emma narrated the story with video blogs and funny posters.

Emma glams up for the 2011 Golden Globe Awards.

CHAPTER THREE

LEADING LADY

Emma and Andrew Garfield (LEFT) try to keep their love on the down low.

One morning in late 2010, Emma's phone woke her out of a deep sleep. The caller was Doug Wald, her manager. Emma was afraid that something horrible had happened. Why else would he call at 5:30 a.m.?

Actually, Doug had amazing news to share. Emma's star turn in *Easy A* had been a big hit. She'd been nominated for a Golden Globe Award!

Emma was officially a superstar on the rise. In 2011, she starred in two more movies, *The Help* and *Crazy, Stupid, Love*. The same year, she was cast as Gwen Stacy, the female lead in *The Amazing Spider-Man*.

Emma + Andrew = <3

On the set of *The Amazing Spider-Man*, Emma had great chemistry with costar Andrew Garfield.

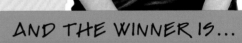

AND THE WINNER IS...

Emma didn't win the Golden Globe for her performance in *Easy A*. But she did win an MTV Movie Award for Best Comedic Performance.

Soon their on-screen romance became a real-life love story. For a while, they tried to keep it a secret. Even though they were both famous, they still wanted their privacy. When reporters asked, Emma told them she just didn't want to talk about her personal life.

But Emma and her new bf couldn't hide from the paparazzi when they went out together. So one afternoon, they decided to take advantage of the unwanted attention. When photographers followed them to take pictures, the couple held up signs. Their message directed people to websites for charitable organizations. One was Gilda's

DOG DAYS

Over the holidays in 2012, Emma and Andrew adopted a dog together. They rescued their golden retriever, Ren, from a shelter.

Emma and Andrew take Ren for a stroll.

Emma and Andrew decided to mix it up with the paparazzi.

Club, a support network for people living with cancer. It was named after Gilda Radner, a comedian Emma admired, who died of the disease.

Celeb-rating a Good Cause

Promoting a website for cancer survivors wasn't a random choice for Emma. Her mom is a breast cancer survivor. As a celebrity, Emma could use her fame to support a cause she really believed in.

EMMA'S FAVS

Actress: Diane Keaton
Band: the Beatles
Book: *Franny and Zooey* by
　　　J. D. Salinger
Food: oysters
Movie: *City Lights*

In 2012, Emma and her mother posed together in a Revlon ad for breast cancer awareness. Emma was interviewed about it, and on this topic, she didn't hold back. She told reporters that when her mother was declared cancer-free, she and her mom got matching tattoos to celebrate.

As Emma explained, their shared tattoo is a small picture of blackbird feet. It stands for the Beatles song "Blackbird," which is about turning negatives into positives. The tattoo was actually drawn by former Beatle Sir Paul McCartney. Emma had met Sir Paul through her *Zombieland* costar Woody Harrelson. Later, she'd written Sir Paul a letter asking him to make the design. Anything for Emma!

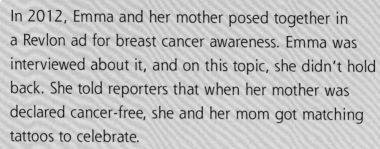

Emma shows off her wrist tattoo.

Paul McCartney was the one celebrity Emma had always wanted to meet. So when she was invited to dinner at his house, she was starstruck! But she loosened up when she and the other guests played party games with their host.

All-Around "It" Girl

Eight years after moving to L.A., Emma was everywhere. She walked the red carpet at the Oscars. She appeared on magazine covers and in ads—not to mention all the movies she made. She joined the star-studded cast of *Gangster Squad*.

Emma starred alongside Ryan Gosling (RIGHT) for the 1940s-era film *Gangster Squad*.

She reprised her role as Gwen Stacy in *The Amazing Spider-Man 2*. She even took the part of a cartoon character, voicing Eep in *The Croods*.

Emma loves acting, of course. But that doesn't mean she has a one-track mind. She bakes to help herself relax.

REPRISE =
a repeat appearance

FAMOUS FRIENDS

Many of Emma's gal pals are as famous as she is. She's tight with singer Taylor Swift (LEFT) and actress Jennifer Lawrence.

FITTING IN FITNESS

Emma hates going to the gym, so she finds other ways to stay fit. Her favs: swimming, rock climbing, pilates (special muscle exercises), and walking.

She loves reading—when she can find the time. She even got into biology when she visited a lab to prepare for her role in *The Amazing Spider-Man*.

One day, Emma may step out of the spotlight. She'd like to get behind the camera and produce her own films. For now, though, she's front and center, living the life of a movie star.

EMMA

PICS!

Emma and Andrew share a laugh at the premiere of *The Amazing Spider-Man* in Madrid, Spain.

SOURCE NOTE

7   "*Saturday Night Live* Clip (Emma Stone Monologue)," IMDb, clip from Hulu.com, televised by NBC on October 23. 2010, http://www.imdb.com/video/hulu /vi2584254745/.

MORE EMMA INFO

Emma Stone Biography
http://www.biography.com/people/emma-stone-20874773
Learn more about the star's life story.

Higgins, Nadia. *Logan Lerman: The Perks of Being an Action Star*. Minneapolis: Lerner Publications, 2014. If you liked reading about Emma, you'll love this fun bio on Logan Lerman—another up-and-coming star of the big screen.

IMDb Emma Stone
http://www.imdb.com/name/nm1297015
Get a complete list of Emma's acting credits.

People, Celebrity Central, Emma Stone Biography
http://www.people.com/people/emma_stone/biography
Travel through an Emma Stone timeline—with pics!

Us Weekly, "Emma Stone's Hair Evolution"
http://www.usmagazine.com/celebrity-beauty/pictures/emma-stones-hair-evolution-2012211/25884
See how Emma's changed her hair color and style over the years.

INDEX

Amazing Spider-Man, The, 21, 27

"Blackbird", 24

Crazy, Stupid, Love, 21

Drive, 17

Easy A, 19, 21

Gangster Squad, 25
Garfield, Andrew, 21–23
Ghosts of Girlfriends Past, 19

Harrelson, Woody, 24
Help, The, 21
Heroes, 18
House Bunny, The, 12, 19

Malcolm in the Middle, 17
Martin, Steve, 9–10
McCartney, Sir Paul, 24–25

New Partridge Family, The, 16–17

Panettiere, Hayden, 18
Paper Man, 19

Radner, Gilda, 23
Rocker, The, 19

Saturday Night Live, 5–7
Stacy, Gwen, 21, 26
Stone, Krista, 15, 23
Superbad, 12, 18

Timberlake, Justin, 6

Wald, Doug, 17, 21

Zombieland, 19, 24

PHOTO ACKNOWLEDGMENTS

The images in this book are used with the permission of: © ROBYN BECK/AFP/Getty Images, pp. 2, 21; © Gregg DeGuire/FilmMagic/Getty Images, pp. 3 (top), 9; © Michael Buckner/Getty Images, pp. 3 (bottom), 16; Johns Pkl/Splash News/Newscom, p. 4 (top left); © Ray Tamarra/FilmMagic/Getty Images, p. 4 (top right); © Fotonoticias/WireImage/Getty Images, p. 4 (bottom); © Florian G Seefried/Getty Images, p. 5; © Dana Edelson/NBC/NBCU Photobank/Getty Images, pp. 6, 7; Seth Poppel Yearbook Library, pp. 8 (top), 11; © iStockphoto.com/JacobH, p. 8 (bottom); Courtesy Everett Collection, p. 10; © Columbia Pictures/Courtesy Everett Collection, pp. 12, 18; Russ Einhorn/Splash News/Newscom, p. 13; © Vera Anderson/WireImage/Getty Images, p. 14 (left); © Mirek Towski/FilmMagic/Getty Images, p. 14 (right); © S_buckley/ImageCollect, p. 15; © 20th Century Fox/Everett/Rex USA, p. 17; © Screen Gems/Courtesy Everett Collection, p. 19; © Alo Ceballos/FilmMagic/Getty Images, p. 20 (left); © Acepixs/ImageCollect, p. 20 (right); © Tom Meinelt/Splash News/CORBIS, p. 22; Felipe Ramales/PacificCoastNews/Newscom, p. 23; © Lester Cohen/WireImage/Getty Images, p. 24; © Warner Bros. Pictures/Courtesy Everett Collection, p. 25; © Kevin Winter/Getty Images, p. 26; © Raymond Hall/FilmMagic/Getty Images, p. 27; © Byron Purvis/AdMedia/ImageCollect, p. 28 (top); © Fotonoticias/FilmMagic/Getty Images, p. 28 (bottom); © Luca Teuchmann/WireImage/Getty Images, p. 28 (right); © Michael Tran/FilmMagic/Getty Images, p. 29 (top left); © Neilson Barnard/Getty Images, p. 29 (center); © Admedia/ImageCollect, p. 29 (right); © Jon Kopaloff/FilmMagic/Getty Images, p. 29 (bottom left).

Front cover: © Nancy Kaszerman/ZUMAPRESS.com/ImageCollect (left); © Dominique Charriau/WireImage/Getty Images (right).

Back cover: © Byron Purvis/AdMedia/ImageCollect.

Main body text set in Shannon Std Book 12/18.
Typeface provided by Monotype Typography.